Newton Mearns
Then and Now
David Pettigrew

The Star Tea Rooms on Main Street were advertised on postcards as being 'near Post Office' and offered 'first class' meals throughout the day at 'moderate prices'. With a smoking room and ladies room, the adverts specifically mentioned catering for cycling clubs and rambling parties, signifying the rural nature of the area at that time.

© David Pettigrew, 2022
First published in the United Kingdom, 2022,
by Stenlake Publishing Ltd.
www.stenlake.co.uk
ISBN 978-1-84033-917-8

The publishers regret that they cannot supply copies of any pictures featured in this book.

Printed by
P2D, 1 Newlands Rd, Westoning, Bedford MK45 5LD

Further Reading

The following were the principal books and websites used by the author during his research. None of the books are available from Stenlake Publishing; please contact your local bookshop, reference library or search for them on the internet.

Anne Loudon and David Kidd, *Old Newton Mearns*, Stenlake Publishing, 2001
Lesley Williams and Anne Loudon, *Mearns Matters*, Stenlake Publishing, 2003
Evening Times
Glasgow South and Eastwood Extra
British Listed Buildings: britishlistedbuildings.co.uk
Gazetteer for Scotland: scottish-places.info
Mactaggart & Mickel: macmicgroup.co.uk
Mearns History Group: mearnshistory.org.uk
Scottish Golf Courses: scottishgolfcourses.com
Old Glasgow Pubs: oldglasgowpubs.co.uk
Youtube.com: 'Vigour Events – Pilmuir Quarry Aquathlon 11th June 2016'

The single storey cottages in the background of this view of Main Street were originally weaver's cottages. Already somewhat dilapidated by the early twentieth century, as can be seen here, by the 1960s Main Street had become severely neglected with several buildings becoming disused; for example by that time the two-storey house on the right and the cottages opposite it had become roofless shells.

Introduction

The earliest significant developments in the parish of Mearns were the building of the castle in the fifteenth century, followed by the kirk and school by the early seventeenth century. These were all based around the original parish centre at Mearnskirk on the original Kilmarnock road, although this became less significant as houses and businesses, including the Newton Inn, appeared on the Ayr road by the early 1800s. Netherplace bleachworks opened in the late eighteenth century though the local economy remained largely based on the many farms in the parish. The nineteenth century saw the opening of two gas works, a post office, two railway stations and the development of some of the original cottages on Main Street into more substantial two-storey properties. Anderson's garage opened in 1902 and Mearnskirk Hospital thirty years later.

Nonetheless, the population remained small until major residential development began at the Broom estate in 1924. House-building, private and local authority, continued and by the 1950s the population had increased to around 6,000. Despite this, the old village centre at Main Street had become more or less derelict by the 1960s. In the early 1970s this area was replaced by a shopping centre, itself upgraded by the early 1990s. Meanwhile substantial housing was created in Crookfur in the 1970s and 80s and in recent years house-building has moved southwards with very substantial developments around the Malletsheugh area.

This book is arranged so that the photographs journey south from the Cross, then north, east and west. It shows the changes and growth Newton Mearns has gone through since the end of the nineteenth century: a visual story of development from a quiet, country community - which had a population of just 900 in 1881 - to the prosperous, busy suburb of over 10,000 homes and 24,000 residents today. With house-building continuing, the story is by no means over.

The William Mann fountain (*see pages 18 and 19*).

The photographs of the exterior and interior of the Bungalow Tearooms on Ayr (previously Kilmarnock) Road were taken around 1905 and were printed on postcards that were probably sold at the establishment. The tearooms were clearly the first stop for visitors as the messages on both postcards state that the correspondents had just arrived.

Now a private home, the building still looks remarkably the same, as does the row of houses on the opposite side of the road, making this area's buildings – constructed in the early 1900s – among the oldest in Newton Mearns.

Kilmarnock (later Ayr) Road, looking north, 1958. The image shows a prosperous, well-tended shopping area and gives a strong sense of what was lost when the shopping centre replaced the buildings on the left. Nonetheless, redevelopment has always been a feature of Newton Mearns' history: notable in its absence is the Newton Inn, the prominent two-storey building that can be seen in earlier views of the Cross in this book.

By 1958 the inn had been replaced by a garage and petrol station, while across the road two-storey shops had replaced the single-storey Union Bank premises that had stood at the Barrhead Road junction. All those buildings have gone and the row of shops on the right are now combined as the premises of Fosters Family Funeral Directors; before Fosters, the building had been occupied by Eric N. Smith, goldsmith, and McLaren and McKechnie, opticians.

Kilmarnock (Ayr) Road, looking south. Robert Anderson's garage (opened in 1902) and the large villa next to it (Anderson's home) were swept away to make the junction for the realigned Barrhead Road, though the villas beyond, built between 1904 and 1906, still stand. This photograph was taken around 1916, before the removal of the wall and the installation of petrol pumps at the front of the garage in 1919.

The business was continued by Anderson's sons after his death in 1937 with the building being altered to create a large car sales showroom the following year. There was a branch garage in Giffnock and by the 1950s the firm employed 130 people. As can be seen by the sign, the garage was a longstanding agent for direct sales and wholesale supply of Humber cars; significant revenue was lost when this ended and eventually the business closed in 1980.

About a mile south of Anderson's garage on the road to Kilmarnock stood Malletsheugh Inn, seen here around 1906. The building seen here – built in 1842 – has been completely swept away, with the A77 being realigned to run right through the site of the right-hand part of it. The current building at this site stands on the position of the inn's garden which was to the rear of the main house on the left. For over a century and a half, the area around the site of the Malletsheugh Inn remained rural until significant house-building to the north, west and east of it began in the late 2010s.

In the nineteenth century Malletsheugh was the place for the first change of horses for the coach from Glasgow to Kilmarnock and by the early 1900s had become a popular stop for local cyclists (today many local cyclists will pass the spot on the cycle path created along the route of the A77). In 1960 Tennents Caledonian took over the premises and in 1971 the company altered them to create a bar-restaurant with off sales and delicatessen. This was eventually replaced by the building that stands today. Trading as an inn continued until the early 2010s; it then became an Indian restaurant before becoming the Royal World Buffet Restaurant.

Originally built in 1795 in the immediate vicinity of Netherplace House, Netherplace works was a cloth-processing operation run by Wallace & Co. and employed around 400 people at the height of its productivity in the 1860s. The works changed ownership a couple of times in the 1980s and 90s and finally ceased production around 2003.

The site then lay derelict, becoming an illegal dumping ground which, in 2017, created a massive fly infestation of homes across Newton Mearns, Giffnock and Clarkston. The remaining buildings were subsequently demolished (note the pile of rubble that can just be seen beyond the fence in the photograph above). In 2020 planning permission was given for the construction on the site of a retirement village containing a care home, flats, houses, shops and facilities for healthcare and leisure.

Pilmuir Mill, Newton Mearns

The mill on Pilmuir Road was possibly built around the time the Pilmuir reservoir was constructed by the Crum family in 1887. This was to help power their mills and dye and printing works in Thornliebank and also Newfield cotton mill, which was based in the area now taken by Rouken Glen Park. From this photograph of the early 1900s, it's clear a local agent for Barr's aerated waters was based here (these would have included 'Iron Brew', introduced in 1901). The buildings seen in the old photo have been replaced by a more recent large house though the mill still stands and has been converted into a dwelling.

Just to the east of this location is the site of Pilmuir Quarry which produced whinstone for road building between 1930 and 1974. Fenced off within private land, the flooded quarry hosted an 'aquathlon' in 2016, with an organiser describing the water quality as 'amazing'. However, since then the place has been described as a 'contaminated, barren death trap' and the local press have reported on incidents of trouble caused there by local youths.

Where the junctions of roads to Eaglesham, Barrhead, Glasgow and Kilmarnock meet, the Cross – seen here around 1916 – was in place by 1832 when the 'New Line' opened (this was the name give to the new road from Eastwood Toll to Kilmarnock). Main Street had already been developed by then and the 'Old Line' was the original route south running from Clarkston to Mearnskirk and beyond. The Newton Inn, one of the best-known hostelries in Renfrewshire, stood prominently on the east side of the Cross.

The inn was built in the 1840s and from 1848 offered horse-coach connections with Crofthead Railway Station – renamed Kennishead (Thornliebank) in 1850 – and later Giffnock Railway Station (three times a day), which opened in 1864. It was also the local posting establishment. By the end of the nineteenth century the inn was run by Thomas Porter and was often known as Porter's Inn. By the 1950s it had been demolished and replaced by a garage.

On the right of this and the photograph on page 16 is Burn Cottage which stood where the Eaglesham Road junction is today. In the early 1900s this was the premises of a dairy shop. Opposite the Newton Inn is the William Mann memorial fountain, now the oldest remaining piece of street furniture at the Cross although slightly moved from its original position shown here. Mann was a partner in a ship-owning company and became a notable county councillor who was very involved in local affairs, financing improved water supply and drainage systems for Newton Mearns.

Mann built Whitecraigs House and was a captain of two local golf clubs – Pollok and Eastwood – though not Whitecraigs across the road from his house as he sadly died in 1905, not long before this opened. His daughter gifted the fountain in his memory and his name is also remembered in William Mann Drive, south-west of the Cross.

This photograph showing the west side of the Cross was taken in the 1950s. By this time the parish church, the roof cross of which can be seen on the skyline, had been built and the block of shops facing onto the road had been rebuilt as larger premises.

The older single-storey building immediately to the left of the car in the old photograph contained the local branch of the Union Bank, which had possibly already been rebadged the Bank of Scotland by the time the photo was taken as the two banks merged in 1955. Its site is now taken by the open concourse immediately in front of the current branch of the Bank of Scotland, shown above.

The origins of Newton Mearns Parish Church can be traced back to a secessionist 'Praying Society' which existed in 1643 and which united with neighbouring societies in Neilston and Eaglesham in 1739. This united congregation built its first church and manse in Main Street in 1743 (*see page 42*) but split soon after due to internal arguments. Eventually, it reunited and the original church was replaced in 1836 by this building on Ayr Road, which could seat 400 people.

In 1938 the church was replaced on the same site by the current parish church which contains date stones and building elements of its predecessors. Opening in 1939, the new church could seat 729 people. The adjacent Memorial Hall was built in 1976.

Since this photograph was taken in the 1950s the clubhouse of Broom Tennis Court has had a clock set into the facing gable and the veranda on the left has been enclosed, while the one on the right has been partially enclosed. The building has also been extended and renamed Whitecraigs Lawn Tennis and Sports Clubs, offering eight tennis courts, three squash courts, a gym and fitness studio and a bar and lounge. As late as the 1920s Broom was an estate lying in the empty countryside between Giffnock and Newton Mearns. Some of the mansions of Whitecraigs had been built by that time (a few can be seen here in the background) and all the land along the length of Kilmarnock Road between these two villages was filled with housing by the 1950s.

The original Broom House, built in 1840 by timber merchants John and Arthur Pollok and lying south-east of the tennis courts, became the private Belmont House School in 1934 and it was in that decade that builders Mactaggart & Mickel built the houses of Broom Estate. The company bought the land in the foreground in 1954 but it was only in late 2020 that it began building the houses of 'Little Broom' on it and the adjacent site of Whitecraigs bowling green. Construction of these new houses was completed the following year.

Whitecraigs House, seen here around 1905, overlooks Ayr Road and was built for William Mann (*see page 18*) around 1898, from a design by H.E. Clifford. Its construction was one of the earliest signs of development in the area, followed by Whitecraigs Station – built in 1903 on the other side of the road, just a short distance north of the house, as part of the Lanarkshire and Ayrshire Railway. In 1905 Whitecraigs Golf Club was established not far south of Whitecraigs House and it was formally opened the following year. The course was designed by William Fernie who also designed the Open Championship Ailsa Course at Turnberry.

It's clear from the old photograph that the house initially enjoyed a peaceful, rural location. This peace disappeared as traffic levels on the road rose throughout the twentieth century. Although matters improved somewhat after the opening of the M77 in the 1990s, as can be seen above traffic remains heavy and constant on the route.

Looking towards the Cross from Eaglesham Road, *c.* 1903. The Newton Inn is just right of centre with the farmhouse of Townhead Farm in the right foreground. The original Barrhead Road is in the background. All the land immediately south of the location shown was eventually taken by houses and the green and club house of Mearns Bowling Club, founded in 1920.

'Townhead' survives as the name of Townhead House which still stands, remodelled, up the lane just beyond the bus stop on the left and also as a road which once bordered the south side of Anderson's garage and is now a cul-de-sac of houses. Eaglesham Road has long since been realigned and now runs right through the site of the farmhouse's front garden. A villa now stands on the site of the farmhouse with Maple Avenue running down between it and the site of the Newton Inn.

Following the route of Eaglesham Road east from Townhead to Mearns and turning south for a few yards on an alternative road to Kilmarnock would bring the traveller here to the cottages of Ward Hill, which stood immediately south of Mearns Parish Kirk.

In the early twentieth century Cairn Duff ran a sweet shop at Ward Hill. According to maps the buildings were still standing in the 1940s but they had been swept away by the following decade. Part of the old wall still stands. The first church at Mearns was recorded in 1186 as part of the monastery of Paisley, though there were probably earlier places of worship here. The current parish church was erected in 1813 and enlarged in 1842 and 1853.

In 1932 a vestry, chancel and session house were added to the church. The manse of 1842 still stands across Mearns Road from the church at the junction with Old Humbie Road.

The house and cottage on the right of the old photograph were gone by the 1950s. Their site is now taken by car parking for the church.

Probably replacing an earlier wooden structure, the approximately 40-feet-high Mearns Castle was built by Lord Maxwell in 1449. In the seventeenth century it housed troops charged with hunting down Covenanters (memorials to whom are scattered across the moors to the south) and the interior was reported to be in a good state of repair in the mid 1800s.

In the early 1970s it became the place of worship for the Maxwell Church of Pollok Street, Glasgow, while a new church building – Maxwell Mearns Church – was constructed immediately adjacent. Although there is a plaque on the castle wall from the days of Renfrew County Council (dissolved in the 1970s) stating that it was restored by Renfrewshire Heritage Committee, the castle itself is no longer open or used. It stands to the rear of Mearns Castle High School which was built in 1978.

SHOPS AT MEARNS CROSS

A view of the Cross from the 1950s, with the junction of Barrhead Road on the left across the road. The building of William Mavers' premises around this time was a sign of redevelopment to come though this building itself was short-lived, being swept away along with its neighbours in 1970 and replaced by the first shopping centre which opened in 1972. By this time Kilmarnock Road had been renamed Ayr Road.

The same view today. Given Newton Mearns' history of change, one can't help wondering how it will look in another fifty years.

This photograph was taken at a position now marked by the entrance to the Asda supermarket within the Avenue shopping centre, a view impossible today and a fact that starkly illustrates the radical changes that have occurred in the 114 years since it was taken. Looking east, the junction with Main Street is on the immediate left, with the Newton Inn and the buildings of Townhead Farm in the central background.

As seen here, this part of Barrhead Road has been realigned a few yards over to the south to run past the shopping centre.

Barrhead Road in the early twentieth century. The field on the left, now taken by the upper level of the west car park serving the Avenue, became the site of the Western SMT bus depot which was in operation in 1932. This was a major employer in the area and there were very frequent bus services to Glasgow, Clarkston, Eaglesham and Ayrshire. The depot was swept away for the shopping centre at the start of 1970s and relocated to Thornliebank. The police station is the building with the Baronial-style facade on the left; the post office was in the white house with the dormer windows two doors up (later there was a branch on Main Street).

This is how this part of Barrhead Road looks today; the original alignment resumes at the junction of Capelrig Road, opposite which stands St Cadoc's RC Church which was built in 1906 (now the premises of Orchard Park Nursery). A hundred and twenty years ago, beyond the western edge of the village it was open countryside to Tofts Bleachworks lying north-west (the site of which is now taken by the houses encircled by Lambie Crescent in Crookfur), and Netherplace, lying south-west. Almost all of this countryside is now taken by housing.

Main Street, looking towards the north around 1905. The building on the right with the dormer windows was the Secession Church, built in 1743 (*see page 22*); the larger manse, built in 1789, is to its right. Both buildings had become shops by this time, the church becoming the premises of J. Elliot's grocers.

Maps show that the main concourse of the Avenue shopping centre runs exactly along the route of the southern part of Main Street.

Main Street, looking south. In the 1930s around 6,000 new houses were built in Newton Mearns along with new blocks of shops on the Kilmarnock (Ayr) Road. This must have shifted local emphasis away from Main Street and it began to fall into dereliction from the 1950s.

Maps of the area from throughout the twentieth century starkly illustrate the extent of this change, the wider area filling with streets of new houses as the decades progress, while gap sites appear in the initially packed Main Street. Without those maps and the photographs that remain, it's hard to imagine this street ever existed.

The tenement building on the right of this view was Newton Place, built to replace a row of thatched weavers' cottages. A Dr Mackinlay, who established his local practice in 1880, built them and so they became known as the 'Doctor's Building'.

Mackinlay was succeeded by Dr Fordyce whose name was given to Fordyce Court sheltered housing on Capelrig Road, just a little way west of the north car park serving the Avenue. The more recently built Capelrig Apartments are right of centre in the background.

The area stretching north-west from Newton Mearns Cross to Patterton Farm (a short distance to the right (west) of this cottage). saw extensive building ot the housing estates of Crookfur in the 1970s and 80s. Out of shot on the left is Patterton Station. This opened on 1 May 1903 and, apart from a brief period of closure during the First World War, serves the area to this day.